POEMS FOR
SUNNY DAYS & UGLY DAYS

An Inspirational Poem for Any Occassion

POEMS FOR
SUNNY DAYS & UGLY DAYS

An Inspirational Poem for Any Occassion

TAMA HENRY

EXTREME OVERFLOW PUBLISHING

EXTREME OVERFLOW PUBLISHING
A Brand of Extreme Overflow Enterprises, Inc.
P.O. Box 1811
Dacula, GA 30019
www.extremeoverflow.com

Copyright © 2024 Tama Henry. All rights reserved.

No part of this book may be reproduced or transmitted in any form or by any means electronic or mechanical photocopying, recording, or by any information storage and retrieval system without the prior written permission of the author, except for the inclusion of brief quotations in critical reviews and certain other noncommercial uses permitted by copyright law.

Published by Extreme Overflow Publishing

ISBN: 0-0-0000000-0

Printed in the United States of America
Library of Congress Catalog in-Publication Data is available for this title

For permission requests, contact the publisher.
Send feedback to info@extremeoverflow.com

DEDICATION

This book is dedicated to my children Chris, Tasha and grandchildren Gabrielle and Charnette with the hope that these words will be wholesome value for their lives in Christ.

Encouraging everyone to find joy as you read these words.

ACKNOWLEDGEMENTS

Thanks to my beloved Savior Jesus Christ with whom I have such a precious relationship. This book with all its contents are directly inspired from Him, who gives me the wisdom, knowledge and understanding to capture and put pen to my thoughts.

To my dear son Christopher who is my encourager and pusher to write relentless in making this to come to fruition. To my wonderful daughter and granddaughter Tasha and Gabrielle who have been the rock to help me to record and document these inspired lines and for encouraging me to never give up.

CONTENTS

Introduction	10
Waiting patiently on God	11
Our Mighty God	12
Give to him your all	13
God is faithful	14
When friends fail you	15
You will laugh again	16
The darkness has recompense	17
It will come to pass	19
Your Boaz is on the way	20
Give to God his part	21
Sow good seeds	22
Children God's gift	23
Right choice right time	24
Your Gift	25
The tongue	26
Mother	27
Pain	28
Empty Bucket	29
Fear	30
A Lady's Bag	31
Mothers eyes	32
The feather in my cup	33
My home is my Castle	34
My Brother Next Door	35
Be encouraged	36
The sun will shine again	37
The Road of Life	38
The end of the road	39
The Chip on the shoulder	41

Keep your chin up	42
The feeble heart	43
The Target	44
Be Faithful	45
A Life of Trust	46
Exchange is no robbery	47
People are people	48
The Judge of all Judge	49
The Author and Finisher	50
Your Character	51
Helping hands	52
Sharing	53
Old Age	54
Words	55
The Flowers	56
The Stars	57
My Pillow	58
The Table	59
Reading	60
Work	61
My Shoes	62
Knock it softly and move on	63
Like A Child	65
What If You are Wrong	67

INTRODUCTION

My heart's desire is to see people read and take counsel from the heart of these poems. These poems were written as living words that can help you turn your dark and ugly days into bright and sunny days.

As you travel through life, this book can be used as a close friend, to talk with, to go to sleep with and to eat with.

The good book says, "Gold there is, and rubies in abundance, but lips that speak knowledge are rare jewels." Proverbs 20:15 NIV

Let this book of poems guide you through your path of life and help you to be the person others can depend on.

WAITING PATIENTLY ON GOD

When you give your life to God,
When you surrender all to him,
And you think you have it all,
Then patiently wait on him.

If answers you are searching,
Lay each question in a row,
Gently place them at his feet,
For there he is waiting now.

Do not take them up while waiting,
Free your back from all its load,
You will find real joy and peace,
As you stand there without doubt.

So wait, the answer is on the way,
Steadfastly keep your eyes on him,
For he takes them all each day,
He sends the answers while you waiting.

OUR MIGHTY GOD

Oh! Mighty God, our God is,
Maker of heaven and earth,
Lover of all mankind, he is,
Giver of all things that is worth.

Are you of God's dear children?
Honor God for his ownership,
Praise him for his greatness,
Thank him for the big three.

He is your friend and comforter,
He is your great healer,
He is your great provider,
Full of goodness forever and ever.

GIVE TO HIM YOUR ALL

Are you tired and feel you are trapped
By the circumstances small or great?
Are you feeling sad and mad,
In a corner out of place?

Bring your heartaches to the master,
He is just the one for you.
He has gifts for every favor,
Caring, looking out for you.

Oh, the love he awaits to lavish,
Upon all who comes his way,
All who give to him their sins,
In exchange for his daily care.

GOD IS FAITHFUL

God is faithful to his promises,
To the rich and to the poor,
To the small and great intent,
Let his faithfulness out pour.

God of mercy, love, and compassion,
Say "yes" to his will,
For all in his own image to stand,
And hope someday to live as one.

Do not be discourage child of God,
When prayers take long to come through,
Gods timing is never wrong,
For our God is ever true.

WHEN FRIENDS FAIL YOU

If friends you once trusted failed you of late,
And you think it's vain to trust anyone,
Look again, you'll find hope in one again.
For a chip is on the shoulder of everyone.

Do you think you are under the table?
Where it is scarcely for someone to be
It's there you will consider and think a little,
Of a place you could better be.

So pick up your feet, raise your hand
Look to the four corners of the earth
Talk to the maker of the land.
Be a friend, for he is yours from birth.

YOU WILL LAUGH AGAIN

When the storm of life is blowing
And the tempest wild and hard;
Ask the good man of the storms a howling
Keep you with a smile at heart.

Only when you have met him before
In the secret place in prayers.
Can your power be restored;
And a sad heart turned to laughter.

Oh how sweet it is to know
You can laugh even through the storm;
For no storm will last forever, no! No!
The Master controls the storm.

THE DARKNESS HAS RECOMPENSE

Don't be afraid when you are in the darkness,
Keep your cool and pray without ceasing,
There you can find peace in the unpleasantness,
As you go through it, courageously and learning.

When you face the darkness of life,
Evaluate your time and space,
What can you do to fill the time,
To make it impactful on the stage of life?

Don't sit back and cry too hard,
Although tears have their part,
Think of the lesson one can have,
In being in the dark.

Gather your thoughts to triumph from there, night to day,
Then after the light comes and darkness disappear,
Bright shining sun in recompense rewarding your life,
You will know how to help another because you have walked that way.

IT WILL COME TO PASS

If you tried and don't succeed at first,
And you feel like it is all done,
Try again and see what it's worth,
As to put your shoulder back, with fun.
Don't stress.

Don't give up nor give in to what they say,
Determine to push and go a head anyway,
Till you hear the inner voice say,
Don't be weary keep going all the way.

It will come to pass as you work and pray,
Do your best with an open heart,
God's mighty hand will lay on you,
And will make it come to pass.

YOUR BOAZ IS ON THE WAY

Do you think you are on the shelf line?
As your age is climbing up,
Remember age is just a thought in time.
When you are down and think you are up.

Your Boaz is on the way dear friend.
Your Boaz is on the way,
Just think of him as you go along.
Prepare yourself, and think of ways,
To make him joyful all the day long.

Life may look dark and maybe unfair,
Hold on you will see it won't last long,
When your dreams come through as fair,
You will forget the time you waited long.

GIVE TO GOD HIS PART

Never take from God his part,
You will find it hard to give back,
What belongs to him today not in part,
He deserves both front and back.

If you don't want to obey his laws,
And to give according to his will,
He will have some other terms,
That you will have to meet.

Give to God his own always,
Do not rob God of his own,
He can take back, by his means, his ways.
What is rightly his, he owns.

SOW GOOD SEEDS

Be careful friend what seeds you sow,
Let them all be true and good,
For seeds do turn and turn and grow,
Though they may be bad or good,
When you sow your seeds each day,
Take a note along the way,
Water them well with love today.
For tomorrow you'll reap just what you sow.

CHILDREN ARE GOD'S GIFT

Love your children they are heritage from God,
They are lent to you, yes everyone,
Soon their own path they will take,
Like a bird they fly out, they fly away.

Remember without notice they will grow up
things may come out
If you train them right with love,
According to God's precious plan,
They will be your joy and make you proud.

Be thankful of God's gift to you'
Take them as your pride and joy,
Even though some are given just a few,
Take heed not to avoid the little few.

RIGHT CHOICE RIGHT TIME

Are you ready to make your choice?
In life there are so many to see,
You must be conscious that you are right,
For when it's done the affect you will meet.

It's good to dream and elevate your mind,
To position your thoughts for your dream to rise.
In time you will see you made the right choice,
A prize you will receive at the right time.

So sit and think, settle down,
For things and actions to take and do,
Because with them all you will have to own,
And live with them all your life through.

YOUR GIFT

God has a gift for everyone,
For you as well as me,
Don't just look at it, you have to use it,
Or else you will find you loose it.

If you don't know what your gift is,
Ask the giver of all creation,
He won't hide from you that thing you need to know,
Because from him it all comes freely with love abound.

So thank God for his goodness, his favor,
For what you have you got from him,
Jesus the great giver, friend and master,
There is much for you as well as me.

THE TONGUE

So small and soft this member is,
Of all the members of the whole body,
It has no bone to break in pieces,
But need not wonder
It's funny, words can break you, you see.

The tongue can set this whole body on fire,
But God the best tamer of this little member.
For no man can tame, even by water,
Only God can shut the mouth dumb.
Even when trouble is caused from what's said and done.

Dear Master, creator of me and all creation,
Help me tame this tongue of mine from peril,
Help us guard it under subjection,
Let us use more of the other little members,
The ears, that listen to empower reaction.

MOTHER

Mother, what a gift that God has given,
To mankind that is good,
It's a gift that is sent from heaven,
May we embrace her awesomeness,
For honor is her claim for your gain.

Love her ever kindly with the finest care,
Reach her with the greatest gift,
Cherish her love with heart so great,

Give her time to accomplish her task
Assigned to her by God the father,
He too has given her jewels of beauty,
Children display the world she harbors.

PAIN

Do not despise your hour of pain,
It is a time with good reason,
Don't matter from where it comes,
Seek to work thru their season.

If there is no pain when you get a cut,
No pain when the leg has broken,
Then you will never know,
That it is ready for healing.

EMPTY BUCKET

There goes the bucket empty and dry,
They say it has no use, its just there,
Taking up space where someone else could stay,
Even left alone it is empty in the same place.

You think you know best for the empty bucket?
You can try to fill it with your own mind,
But it is only meant to make all the noise.

For an empty bucket makes the most noise.

FEAR

When you become timid and fearful,
And feel like it's best to blow up in panic,
Remember the feeling is a passing emotion,
So do what is best to let it go out.

Don't sit down and nurse fear,
For its cousin doubt will come too close.
For when doubt and fear join hands,
They create havoc.
If you let them have their fun, they just won't care.

Starve your fear with more faith,
You will overthrow both fear and doubt.
Ask the author, the one who is pleased by faith,
To banish the fear and doubt your doubt.

A LADY'S BAG

She packed her bag with diligence,
With everything she would need,
Leaving out, not a single item,
Though sometimes in rush she would leave.

Then when she would lose a pen,
She would search the whole bag from end to end
And still can't find it then,
Unless the whole bag is turned upside down and shaken.

MOTHER'S EYES

A mother's eyes can see far away,
Further, than any other normal person can,
They can see incoming danger quicker,
Than the eyes of a normal man.

Her eyes are like the eagle's eyes,
Even as they soar from far distance,
And when she is around each will find,
That the home is happy as a lark.

She has hope and trust when looking,
Whether night and day it's all the same,
God gave her this special instinct,
Of the eyes like an eagle's flame.

THE FEATHER IN MY CAP

I wander day to day on a beautiful trail,
With my special decorated white cap,
It's the feather from the pea-cocktail,
My hat is now a beautiful wonder on top.

I love the beauty that it is showing,
From east west north and south on top mi hat,
That's the way each child should be,
Like a feather in parents hat.

Little boys and girls, think big and do well,
Of the things to cultivate a beautiful mind,
To make your parents head radiate,
Like a peacock striding proud all the time.

MY HOME IS MY CASTLE

I saw a large and beautiful house,
On the other side of town, it's so great!
The owner must be rich, maybe famous,
To have their name signed to this great place.

This must be a place called Castle.
With beauty and glamour to behold,
But fussing and fighting bellows from inside that castle,
Even though there are riches untold.

I have my home-made castle too,
Though not as large and beautiful as this,
But love and harmony flow true,
I am proud of my home, my castle, my peace.

MY BROTHER NEXT DOOR

When you look with innocents next door and see a man,
Who does not dress with looks profound,
He may not have nice things like you have nice things,
But he is your brother just next door.

He may be scrawny, talk bad with broken words,
Listen to him he may need your converse,
Just to chat a while that's what it's worth,
He is your brother, few in words but count a mighty worth.

Don't distance the man you see next door,
Maybe 2moro you may need his helping hand,
Do what you can for him the more,
For he is your brother next door.

BE ENCOURAGED

Are you discouraged over life right now,
Do you feel like throwing in the towel,
Have you said to yourself, "I am done,
There is nothing left for me to be done."

Remember the word, hope,
Keep it alive and sing on your way,
For hope never fails as you go,
Take up fresh courage forever, be brave.

You will find each time you push on through,
Your hope gets stronger, your will to go through,
For the courage to go is stronger than all the refused,
It's the hope of the view and the courage to pursue.

THE SUN WILL SHINE AGAIN

Oh! It's dark and gloomy a good while now,
I wonder when it will be sunny again,
With bright arrays, lighting up the surround,
The dark clouds depart and the light shines again.

Give thanks for the days when it was sunny,
Give thanks now for the dark gloomy days,
All of them go together to make up a life story,
And to make a variety of life's sunny days.

So don't curse the darkness for it will soon change,
And things will come back to normal again,
The sun actually shines each and every day,
Let your heart be thankful each day just the same.

THE ROAD OF LIFE

It is one step at a time on the road of life,
So don't hurry or else you will slip and slide,
It's easy to fall if your steps are not firm and right,
Walk good my friend, care not to slide.

But if you happen to fall as others do,
Brush yourself off and start again from that lesson,
For the race is not for the swift and strong,
But to him that endures at best to the end.

Take note sometimes you may go alone with God,
When on the road of life as you travel along
Because others often bring torment and woe,
But with God, don't wonder about Life's worth.

THE END OF THE ROPE

Imagine, a virtuous man who once walk the talk,
Now has turned far away, no sign of him stop drinking,
Retracing his steps to the same rum bar, Visiting,
Call it madness, you may, the same results will happen
Same every time he comes back drunk from the bar Visiting

My patience goes weary enduringly,
For what to do next I don't know,
Should I stay away, it's not the virtue I imagine,
When I stay, it's a havoc, big fussing and quarreling,
Lord I feel I reach the end of the rope.

There there now my child, if this sings your song,
And you want the virtuous man to stop drinking,
Quit yearning, bend your knees and do praying the most,
God always answer, he can stop the hunger for intoxicating
God's love is longer than rope.

THE CHIP ON THE SHOULDER

Everyone has a chip on the shoulder,
I may not know yours and you may not know mine,
It may be large, it may be small,
But it still spells chip and that is for sure.

Don't distress yourself we are all human beings,
We all will fall, when we fail then we begin,
We end up with cuts and bruises that sting,
You look in the mirror, you may hate what you see.

Please do recognized your chip,
You think you are the worst of all,
Brush yourself off, despite your chip,
You will make it and walk through the famous hall.

KEEP YOUR CHIN UP

Keep your chin up says the older folks,
You are not done yet there is still time enough,
Hold your head high there is much to unfold,
For you have your part in this life though tough you know.

Your role is your part you must not neglect,
For no one can do that for you as you would yet,
So try, muscle up, steam up, and go hit your target,
To this end you must prevail with the right mindset.

Encourage who struggle with heads bowed down,
To hold up heads high, you ain't no clown,
There is much great gain in an upward bound,
A mouth humming to God with chin up without a frown.

THE FEEBLE HEART

How many a heart get feeble and low,
As they face the ills and troubles of life,
They struggle along and search for good energy flow,
As they hope for the help that will bring them true life.

Take heart and keep courage along the way,
You must not be defeated and let down,
Your heart is alive and you can still say,
I can get up and try without doubt,

Thank Jesus, the hope, determination and desire,
To look at life in a different direction,
Where dreams turn to vision, the reality of ideas
To push you in front of your discouraging reaction.

THE TARGET

Yes, it seemed you are the target the enemy has,
He rolls you over and over – bullseye
He picks you up and throws you like a toy,
As if he owns you and you are his fan.

You may be easy but you are no fool,
Be wise and think straight in the dust,
Next when you look up and out of the blue,
Let him know you are not done if you must.

You are a God kind, mankind, his blood in your vein,
You won't be target practice for the enemies fame
Do your purpose, impact large or great,
For you are the only one made with, umph, to
Conquer this here trail.

BE FAITHFUL

It's hard to be faithful when others are not so,
Some skimping and scamming and life so great,
It's hard to be faithful when only you are being true,
And standing upright when others fail to demonstrate.

Each man has a time to stand tall and strong,
No matter who packs and leave saying so long,
Your task is to be there, time does not rehearse,
And see your work done to the very last.

Trod straight my friends, obey the golden rules,
Rely on the Lord's Book, there lies the best guide,
Let no one detour you away from the truth,
Till your stretched hands receive rewards with delight.

A LIFE OF TRUST

I look to the right and then to the left,
I sob and I cry, longing for a friend,
Someone on whom I can depend,
Just to hold my hand as I hope for the best.

Yes, there is one I can lean on and hope,
When he hears my voice, when I call out for help,
He listens, takes notes, help me step,
To walk out of problems and step off the stress

So, if life is empty, trust Jesus to fill it,
Keep fully trusting him for overflowing,
For he who has promise is faithful to do it,
He is faithful overrunning.

EXCHANGE IS NO ROBERY

Have you ever given away treasure for something?
Feels like a game and if it's worth it all,
The path is not known, will it ever be?
Striving for your cause, exchange by Sunday

Anchor your heart, it may be rough for the one,
To whom you try to exchange a thing or two,
Time passes, don't give up you won't be robbed,
This is not a game, you will not lose.

Look up it's not over it's not done yet,
Focus to favor your coast to enlarge for you,
For that which you have given in exchange,
Behold more than expected out of the blue.

PEOPLE ARE PEOPLE

As you travel along life's road each day,
You will come across all types of people,
Some may love you and let you feel wanted,
Others may hate you and you feel subservient.

Let's find out who are the caring people,
Just lay by the roadside, act like you're hurting.
Then you find out who are, Samaritan gospel,
For people are people and that's no joking.

So, try your best as you live your life through
Treat others as you would like them to treat you.
Be kind, be honest be loving and true,
People are people you might need help too.

THE JUDGE OF ALL JUDGES

Things go around like gossip, and you judge,
Just query each thought before say oh!
For the same measure you use you judge,
No doubt it will be dealt right back to you.

You don't have to play big and powerful,
Everyone should be kind and humble.
The day your hands lift to fight, that's awful!
The hand of that judge you cannot fight.

Therefore go easy with each other my friend,
Don't forget we are all weak doers,
And need each other maybe soon, ah well!
The Judge of all judges is right at the door.

THE AUTHOR AND FINISHER

He who begins the race must finish it,
In life we fall and get back up each day
The clock still ticking, dropping out it's still ticking
Because each man must run his own race.

The road may be rough and thorny,
Follow the authors' plan, like a Sergeant Master,
You'll find his yoke is easy, he has his own army,
Rest, as your author's burden is pleasantly light.

Keep in touch with your author,
He will cause you to finish well,
For he is your author and finisher,
He won't stop until all is well.

YOUR CHARACTER

Your character is just who you are,
As you develop who you are each day,
In tough times and in places far,
You build your own self with the sense of faith.

Don't feel bad or dismay in different hours,
You may not know but your character will take you higher,
To have you climb the path that leads to honor,
Just train your lips and say this won't last forever.

Protect who you are though difficult it may be,
The obstacles you see today they too are stepping stones,
To propel you to be the purpose like a seed,
The character that others may want to capture.

HELPING HANDS

Many have been released with too lovely hands,
To do all the good that need to be done,
For everybody needs some helping hands,
To help them soon before they are gone.

They will need a hand to lift them up,
From the depth of discouragement and pain,
They may even hang their head in shame.
Helping hands are fuel to be brave

So dear friends teach your hands to be ready,
To lend a helping hand to those who are lame;
For the hand you lend today that's ready,
May be the very hand you will need someday.

SHARING

What I have is for me myself and I,
My life would be like the dead sea,
Which takes in all and have no outlet,
Then other may perish because all I have kept

The world is in need for something I keep,
I could share and let someone else be happy,
With things I have more than I would need,
For the needs they have are more than heavy.

Turn away from your selfishness and greed,
Instead of yourself alone adopt a giving heart,
When you share with others you will see,
That the door is open to release more to you.

OLD AGE

It is a beauty to grow old with gracefulness,
With love patience, peace and good will.
When the heart is centered on God's perfectness,
Good health and strength will be his will.

Keep heart and mind on everything good,
Let your hands find worthwhile things
That is nice to be about,
And keep in touch with a friend or two,
As you say a prayer for everyone you know.

It is good to grow old after all and all,
Then you will realize all that is wise,
For you would have gone all the ways as they will,
All for you to give them good advice.

WORDS

They say word is wind but that's not true,
The words you speak have great effect on you and
They either are for good or bad outcome,
Because they are hidden somewhere just waiting
To come true.

Words are powerful actors they don't miss,
Just what your tongue tell, angels always do,
They never omit or delete or twist,
Bad and good angels take your words and do.

Words, take thought to your words,
They will lift you up or embarrass you,
For you they must obey in all their works,
They will set you ablaze or place laughter on you.

THE FLOWERS

Flowers are one of the beauties of God's art,
They beautify the earth in various ways,
They capture our hearts and bring us to awe,
In view of the awesomeness to the creators handy work.

Look at the colors neatly fixed and matched,
They cheer the hearts of the sick with hope a new,
They bless the days of the human years with nod,
And give a lovely feeling with so sweet their perfume.

Let's gather them small and great with care,
To beautify our dwellings with hope and serenity,
To give a different sense of love that's dear,
Displaying friendship, beauty and good cheer.

THE STARS

Twinkle do the stars that shine so bright,
To give the world the light it needs,
To brighten someone darkest night,
And disappear as the day meets the night.

The stars owe someone else a start,
You think it's the one who hitches his wagon to the skies,
For if he falls he will not go far,
Because he does not aim for the highest heights.

Oh! Star holder, creator, look and notice far,
Above the skies as beautiful and blue,
Hold on to your dreams with your farthest star,
And depend on the one who fashion you.

MY PILLOW

Soft, comfortable and nice.
To have comfort like this,
Cushion to my sweet dreams,
To lay my head upon a soft rest of slumber,
My pillow and I we journey,
I sleep like a dreamer.

My pillow hears the groans I make,
It sees the tears, the falling tears,
It knows when I fall to sleep, and stay awake,
And no one else ever sees nor hears.

If my pillow could talk everyone would know,
The sorrows and problems I share with it,
Sometimes fast and sometimes deep and slow,
But it is all between where my head and pillow meet.

THE TABLE

It has four legs but cannot walk,
You have to go to it as often as you are able,
For resting things down, eat drink, talk and sit around,
There is no better place to be than at the table.

Around the table You have your family close conversation,
You learn to put in the necessary missing words,
Here you learn to correctly use utensils,
You hear the gossip the stories even the tale of two cities.

Oh, wow, that is intriguing!

Sometimes around the table is full,
With dad mom brother uncle aunt, the whole family,
But remember check the table for a seat for another too,
For the special seat designated to Jehovah Jireh,
Our provider.

READING

It is true that reading maketh a full man,
And confidence in a man makes ready for the right action,
It is true that reading gather treasures in bonds,
And awaits the time to use them with caution.

As you read do make full proof of understanding,
So to remember more of what is written,
To read again and to others you may be telling,
The evidence of the beautiful contents.

Never stop reading good books,
There is knowledge, wisdom and understanding,
To gain in life and nuggets to capture truth,
As you take your stand and always aiming high.

WORK

If work done by hands has any good reward,
Then do it clean and clear with a loving mind set,
For when you have your work cut out grand,
Its good to be alive and at your very best.

The work you wish to do each day,
May be unlike the one you must accept,
You may have to stand on one leg today,
Before you can stand on both at their best.

Be conscious and think real good,
Before you pick, choose, refuse and leave,
For someone will fit in where you could,
And be happy to fill in for the need.

MY SHOES

Can you try to walk a mile in my shoes,
To feel how it feel as I travel on my way,
It may seem easy, comfy and real dandy,
But my shoes won't fit, for it wasn't made for you.

You may look for one just like them,
They may even look alike at its best,
The proof is there when you try to fit them,
But awe the aches and pain that must be felt.

So dear loved ones as you see me hipping and hopping,
Or you may see me going along with lowered head,
It's because of the burdens I am carrying,
And the shoes with a back that is bent.

KNOCK IT SOFTLY AND MOVE ON

(Dedicated to Chris)

When you start and things go wrong,
Knock it softly and move on,
If at all your fingers cannot knock,
And your wrist is tight as knot,
Use your elbow it its strong,
Knock it softly and move on.

Knock it softly brother,
Knock it softly sister,
If success is a must to be won,
You knock it softly and move on,
Think of someone standing by,
Saying to you go on you have the strength to go on.

It may seem everyone passes you by,
And you are destined to come dead last,
Remember the race is not for the swift, "don't sigh",

Neither the battle for the strong, "don't log,"
Just endure and success will come,
Knock it softly and move on.

Are there barriers in your every way,
Slips and slides do mark your tracks?
There's a guideline to mark your way,
Prayers from a million miles way back,
Mother's knees are always bend,
For the ones to her God sends,
You will have no lack.

LIKE A CHILD

Like a child, I come to you,
Like a child I surrender my heart to you,
Wash me whiter than snow,
I repent, come and stay,
Your will today I pray.

Dear Author of life,
This is my moment on your time,
I hope you are not too busy,
I am asking your forgiveness,
Lord let me say, I'm sorry,
Your love is free,
Your love is more than the air I breathe,
I gladly accept your shadow Almighty.

Like a child, I come to you,
Like a child I surrender my heart to you
Wash me whiter than snow,
I repent, come and stay

Your will today I pray,

Please break these chains off me,
My folly, my shame are bounding me,
These odds won't set me free,
To live your way, oh God I know you see,
Give me power to say chains loose from me!
I say chains break asunder from me!

Like a child, I come to you,
Like a child I surrender my heart to you,
Wash me whiter than snow,
I repent, come and stay,
Your will today I pray.

Come purify, come sanctify,
Relentlessly I need you divine,
Though I live under bridges,
Feeding hand to mouth from charity,
You assure me better days foretold,
By the cross, my statue of liberty.

Like a child, I come to you,
Like a child I surrender my heart to you,
Wash me whiter than snow,
I repent, come and stay.
Your will today I pray.

WHAT IF YOU'RE WRONG

I know what I know,
I believe it is true,
I trust what I know, I know,
My understanding is the rock I know,
Compare to all others the better I know.

My friend, your understanding is finite to your brain
In all that you know WHAT IF YOU'RE WRONG?

I believe the doctrine,
And the following of Selassie,
How could he not be, not just because he look like me
The book spoke of him,
From the threshing floor of Jerusalem,
Direct lineage to the king,
With the sling who slay the giant to win,

But my friend, you still have a problem,
Can your belief save your soul?
It's apart of you, you know.

My friend, Oh my friend, WHAT IF YOU'RE WRONG?

I believe in all my gods, a god for every occasion,
400 plus of them you know, oh yes I have all basis covered,
I remember them all, I don't need a rolodex,
I dance the classics,
and please the gods through all my senses,
But my friend, are you sure you have all basis covered?

Like your sin debt with all dem gods with all them faces
A question that can't be answered,
Not even by the BIGGEST rolodex.
My friend, oh my friend, WHAT IF YOU'RE WRONG?

I meditate day and night,
To reach great enlightenment,
To see beyond the realm beyond,
To what the image would have me see,
I burn my incense, to the one great image,
Now I can see, I can see, what I pray to.

Take heed my friend,
Enlightenment must rid you of darkness,
Hence the light of a love supreme,
The love supreme,
Again, my friend, take heed,
Because WHAT IF YOU'RE WRONG?

I am firm in my stance
To follow the belief of the east,
To follow the rules and pray,
More than 3 times a day with ease,
My dear friend,
You are on a path that must answer,
IF you're right or wrong,
I know you don't want to be the weakest link,
So, WHAT IF YOU'RE WRONG?

I believe in creation, not some so-call creator
I can't see him anyways,
I can't have nothing to declare,
All my senses come alive,
To ravel in all creation,

I love touch see smell,
My utopia is epic end to end,
Wait, wait, wait!
There, there now.
Who's air you breathing then?
Where were you when nothing was everything
Who was before the creation?
Who created something out of nothing?
Who was there before it all began?
Let's get real, my friend, WHAT IF YOU'RE WRONG?

If YOU'RE WRONG you will find out,
like a sudden death game plan in a tournament,
There must be a winner a looser,
To bring the game to an end,
But the end is not the end but the beginning of eternity,
Be all the more diligent,
To make your calling and election sure,

Your spirit will never die,
Right or wrong eternity your spirit will live on,
And may Heaven help us all
Anything anyone can lead to obsolete,
But absolute is never wrong.

Choose non comparable, go for not equal to
Jesus The Christ the absolute winner man
The door to secure your spirit the beginning at your end
My friends search yourselves,
DO YOU WANT TO BE WRONG?

Made in the USA
Middletown, DE
21 July 2024